# FROM ONE LOVER'S HEART
# TO ANOTHER

## FORTY SUFI POEMS

By Maissa Hamed

www.enjoyislam.net

Cover design: James Salser

# DEDICATION

To my beloved mother for her inner and outer beauty, joviality, infinite charm and wisdom, whose massive brain hemorrhage on 24 September 1997 and death soon afterwards, marked the birth date of our eldest son and my birth as a poet with the first poem in this anthology: "Birth and Death."

To my beloved father, from whom I inherited among many other things, a love of poetry and whose monumental work producing the first ever rhyming translation of the Holy Qur'an[1] — which my late grandfather Ahmad Hamid started in the 30s — has had a profound impact on me, especially as I had the honor of assisting him with its production and dissemination.

---

[1] Hamid, Ahmad and Hamed, Mohamed. *Meaning of the Holy Qur'an translated into English*. Cairo: Dar El Shorouk, 2011. Print. Read more here http://enjoyislam.net/quran_in_rhyme.html

*From One Lover's Heart to Another: Forty Sufi Poems*

# CONTENTS

# ACKNOWLEDGMENTS

*"He has not thanked His Lord,
he, who has not thanked people."*

Prophet Muhammad,[2]
*Salla Allahu alayhee wa sallam,*
Peace and blessings of Allah be upon him, pbuh.[3]

I am utterly grateful for the myriad of blessings *Allah Subhana wa Ta'ala*[4] bestowed upon me, among which is the success He granted me in publishing my second book you are about to read after the first one, *The Last Night of Ramadan*[5], illustrated by my dear husband, Mohamed El Wakil, AIA,[6] was published in 2007.

There are countless people whom I wish to thank. I apologize if I couldn't mention everyone due to space limitations. To everyone who has paused to read one of my poems, reflect on it, and share your feedback, I start with you all and acknowledge my sincere gratitude. I hope it was a transformative encounter, rekindling a truth forgotten or awakening an emotion, buried deep, that would have otherwise remained unacknowledged.

[2] Hadith (saying) of Prophet Muhammad *Salla Allahu alayhee wa sallam, Peace & Blessings be upon him, pbuh.* Sayings of Prophet Muhammad, pbuh, are known as (Ahadith), which are the Prophetic Traditions or *Sunna*. They are the actual words of the Prophet, and became a science taught in universities. Together the Ahadith and the Qur'an constitute the two main sources of guidance for Muslims. The Ahadith are authenticated by narrators and traced back to the Prophet, through a very detailed chain of transmission back to the Prophet himself.

[3] Traditional salutation following the name of the Prophet Muhammad, pbuh.

[4] Traditional magnification following God's Name, meaning 'Praise be to Allah, The Most Exalted'.

[5] Hamed, Maissa. Illustrated by Elwakil, Mohamed. *The Last Night of Ramadan.* Great Barrington: Bell Pond Books, 2007. Print.

[6] American Institute of Architects

*From One Lover's Heart to Another: Forty Sufi Poems*

I wish to thank all my students of Enjoy Islam[7] and their families who, over the past thirteen years, have given me the highest responsibility of all – namely, their trust to hold their hands, as a humble guide, on the spiritual path. To my teen and adult students, Muslim and Non-Muslim, I wish to extend sincere gratitude, what an honor it has been to serve you all. This anthology of poems and their subtly embedded Islamic wisdoms and mystical teachings is my humble gift to you, as you embark on your own spiritual journey.

Thanks to what has become a haven of love, my *Sohba*, – a spiritually nourishing Qur'an reading circle of now seventy-six members spread out across twenty-two countries, which I have been blessed and honored to establish and serve for over six years now. I thank every *Sohba* member for embracing each new poem, as a gift of love from my heart to yours.

Thank you dear Yusuf Garda for your endorsement which appears on the back of this book. Thank you for reading and commenting on each new poem, no matter how late it arrived on your computer screen in South Africa from New York you promptly read it and hailed its arrival with your wit and expansive knowledge - that of a true literary critic - despite how busy you were publishing your book.[8]

Thank you Khudeja Pochee for publishing my poem: *Only When*, in *The Muslim Woman Magazine*[9] you founded and thank you for the invitation to contribute regularly to your magazine.

---

[7] www.enjoyislam.net

[8] Garda, Yusuf C. *Literature, Life and Cricket: Tales of Fietas.* Cape Town: African Lives in Association with the Gauteng Cricket Board, 2017. Print.

[9] Hamed, Maissa M. "Only When" The Muslim Woman Magazine. 10, Nov. 2017: Vol 18. Print.

Sheriffa and Suleiman Minty, I am grateful to you both for putting me in touch with your South African network as well as for your support and love during the many years we have known you since my husband and I had the pleasure of meeting you both on Hajj in 2008.

Dale Bennett, thank you for your endorsement at the back of this book and for being a mountain of support throughout the birth of this anthology, with your encouraging and piercing commentaries. You encouraged me to keep writing and thanks to your nourishing reassurance, I did. Above all, thanks for being my editor, when I needed another pair of eyes, to look in detail at my manuscript and catch anything I missed or overlooked.

I thank all my friends from various parts of the world. I particularly thank my dear husband, Mohamed Elwakil and our sons, Zain Edeen Elwakil and Noor Edeen Elwakil, for always listening, savoring and sharing your feedback on each new poem I excitedly brought you, minutes after I put down my pen or cursor to rest. Thank you Zain for your meticulous reworking on my logo to make sure it is of the highest quality for publishing on Amazon.

Thank you, James Salser, for your most valuable assistance with cover design and making my manuscript meet the technical requirements for Amazon publishing. I knew I could always count on you. Thank you Lisa Greissinger and Pamela F. Hunt for your love and support.

I thank my father, Mohamed Hamed, for always lending my poems a listening ear and a contemplative heart. Your monumental life achievements which we are blessed to celebrate together, provided great material to write about.

Last, but far from least, I wish to thank my spiritual teacher(s) who have enlightened for me the spiritual path of Love, hence quenching my thirst for a meaningful spiritual existence. Namely, thank you Mawlana Shaykh Hisham Kabbani - a true beacon of light for tens of thousands of spiritual seekers around the world. My family and I are blessed to know you and to be in your radiant presence. We are so grateful you are part of our lives. You have supported me in the hardest of moments and you continue to teach me every day. Thank you Shaykh Abdul Jalil Steffen Stelzer for all your love and support and for always being there for me, my husband and children. Thank you Imam Feisal Abdul Rauf. I learnt a lot from you, for which I will always be grateful.

If the embedded wisdoms and mystical teachings woven delicately in this first humble collection of spiritual poems, *From One Lover's Heart to Another: Forty Sufi Poems* touches your heart, I would be delighted to hear from you. You can reach me through my website: www.enjoyislam.net or by email at mhamed@enjoyislam.net.

May *Allah Subhana wa Ta'ala*, The Exalted, accept and bless this modest effort. May He always guide us, to the transformative path of love. May Allah's Peace and Blessings be upon His beloved Prophet and Messenger, Muhammad, seal of Prophets, who showed us through his own beautiful example and life story, how love conquers hearts.

# INTRODUCTION

*"He loves them and they love Him."*

<small>Holy Qur'an[10]</small>

When the mystical poet's racing emotions settle on paper, the poet's soul enters a comfort zone, as it attempts to escape the decadence of material earthly existence and transcend to the presence of its Beloved, in search for signs, for meaning, in an attempt to restore itself to its natural state of goodness and beauty, on which *Allah Subhana wa Ta'ala* created it. The poet's pen starts flowing, igniting a powerfully creative, meditative process, highly revealing, enlightening and spiritually therapeutic, not just for the poet, but for others as well, who are part of the same human narrative. One can sense a common thread between the mystical poet's pen, the dervish's whirl, or the Islamic Calligrapher's pen, all of whom through *dhikr* – Divine Remembrance –, enter into elevated spiritual states. From that station, certain wisdoms and truths are revealed and knowledges illuminated, which in turn create a sense of calm and tranquility, that emanate from the meditative state of being in dhikr. Writing for me, is part of my spiritual journey. This work is a humble attempt, to use the power of poetry, to express lasting transformative mystical messages in reaction to life's events on the personal and the world stage.

Poetry has always been used to express intense and complicated emotions. William Wordsworth mentions that "Poetry is the spontaneous overflow of powerful feelings; it takes its origin from emotion recollected

---

[10] The Holy Qur'an, 5:54.

in tranquility.[11] 7th Century Arabia, was a haven for poets as they occupied the highest social ranks in Arab Meccan society and hence they were the most esteemed. The most profound of Arabic poetry, that has been written, is *Al Burda*, by the 13th century Egyptian Sufi mystic Imam Al Busiri, which he composed in *Mamluk* Egypt, in praise of the most noble character of Prophet Muhammad, *Salla Allahu alayhee wa sallam*. It is still passionately chanted until today by millions around the globe.

My humble poems reflect my own experience of joy, pain or turbulence regarding the human condition, that profoundly touch my heart and soul deep, moving me to employ my pen, in an attempt to contemplate, reflect, rejoice, heal and soothe, through the enchanting power of poetry. They are all infused by Islamic wisdoms and teachings as per the Holy Qur'an and the Ahadith of Prophet Muhammed, *Salla Allahu alayhee wa sallam*. Giving birth to them is hard, as I try to make sense of my own story and that of others. They reflect the emotional heat brewing inside. They are, like any new birth, packed with pain and hard labor, followed by the usual joy accompanying the new born. The intention behind them is transformative in that they draw heavily on the two true sources of tranquility and peace for hearts truly in submission – Islam – namely dhikr - Remembrance of God and contemplating on the Prophetic Ahadith – sayings of Prophet Muhammad, *Salla Allahu alayhee wa sallam*.

Hence, they are meant to change something in the reader, stirring him/her into contemplation, which is a form of worship in Islam. They aim to provide insight, highlight a forgotten reality, or illuminate heavenly signs from above, the remembrance of which

---

[11] William Wordsworth Quotes." BrainyQuote.com. Xplore Inc, 2018. 14 May 2018. https://www.brainyquote.com/quotes/william_wordsworth_390135

can help in the transformation of the soul, to higher spiritual and moral grounds, thereby transcending the mundane narrative of our material earthly existence and entering into that comfort zone of being in Divine remembrance. Only then, do we experience a sense of awakening, healing and nourishment. This is when transformation occurs and the Divine lover's soul enters another state – a state of being a recipient of Divine Love through dhikr, the remembrance of God - The Beloved. For indeed; "it is with the remembrance of God, that hearts feel calm."[12]

Sufis are trained to focus on the purification of the heart, to serve; to alleviate people's suffering and wipe away their tears, even when they themselves cry, hence, *From One Lover's Heart to Another: Forty Sufi Poems* was born. Unlike other books, this book can be read in several ways. The poems can be read in ascending or descending order (2018 – 2000) or selected at random, as each poem stands alone, as we all will, on the final day.

May this anthology of Sufi poems serve its transformative intention for seekers on their spiritual journeys, in pursuit of Divine Love, which is the only path by which humanity can progress and heal itself of the spiritual maladies of our times: ignorance, hate, greed, envy, jealousy, selfishness and ingratitude among many others. May our hearts be transformed by love - the most powerful emotion that we are blessed with - by the source of Love, *Al Wadud*,[13] The Loving One - all praise and thanks to Him, *Allah Subhana wa Ta'ala* – Lord of the worlds. May we be among those fortunate ones who *Allah Subhana wa Ta'ala* describes in the Holy Qur'an as, "He loves them and they love Him."[14]

[12] The Holy Qur'an, 13:28.
[13] One of Allah's *Subhana wa Ta'ala* divine Names and Attributes.
[14] The Holy Qur'an 5:54

*"Our residence in this phenomenal world is transitory; it is a journey towards the Eternal One. The most miserable man, is he who prefers for himself the material above the spiritual, for the material, apart from its ephemeral nature, obstructs our passage to the spiritual world. Man should not disregard any means to protect himself against all human vices, and he should seek to rise to the highest ends of human virtues…, that is, to the knowledge by means of which we protect ourselves against spiritual and bodily disease, and acquire the human virtues in whose very essence goodness is grounded."*

*The Famous Muslim Scholar Al Kindi, 9th Century.*[15]

Maissa Hamed
1439/2018
New York

---

[15]"Rasa'il al-Kindi al-falsafiya." www.muslimheritage.com. i. 280; in G.N.Atiyeh, Al-Kindi, Rawalpindi: Islamic Research Institute, 1966, p. 127.

# FROM ONE LOVER'S HEART
# TO ANOTHER
## FORTY SUFI POEMS

1.  ## Lovers' Hearts

Lovers' hearts,
As plants, to survive,
They turn to The Light.

Their food,
For their tired souls,
Tastes best, in the heart of the night.

They well know,
No change and no power,
Except through His Might.

Their consciousness,
Is all the time with Him,
Though He is to them, out of sight.

But in every lover's heart,
He dwells,
And Guides, to what's right.

They sing His praises,
Love one another,
And never fight.

O! their times with Him,
Are the most enriching,
The most bright.

In seeking His pleasure,
And His remembrance,
Those lovers' hearts, delight.

Ask them about His Signs,
Around them, and
In themselves, many they could cite.

Long verses of praise,
And humble gratefulness,
They compose and eloquently write.

They cry over the state,
Of their fellow humans,
And pray for their plight.

Lovers' hearts never sway,
From His presence,
Lest they feel constricted and tight.

They love each other's company,
And to their garden of love,
Similar hearts they invite.

Special knowledges,
In lovers' hearts,
The Almighty will alight.

From them you will learn,
How to speak, to love,
To be kind and to live light.

Their purity and polish,
Is infectious, and in your seeking heart,
The spark of love they'll ignite.

Stay long in their company,
And with humility, learn from them,
As you embark on your spiritual flight.

Then you will be forever,
Transformed by Love,
And a deeper insight.

Lovers' hearts,
As plants, to survive,
They turn to The Light.

"Lover's Hearts"
2018

## 2. What Can I Say

What can I say,
When many words are
Better left unsaid.

Emotions that have
No words to describe,
Can still be sensitively read.

Ignoring them,
For pretense sake
Is hypocrisy I dread.

Your words and deeds,
Will stay alive,
After you're dead.

Choose them carefully,
As it is joy, peace and calm
You should spread.

When the dark clouds
Of arrogance and stubbornness hit,
You must carefully tread.

Have you ever felt the coldness
And chills through your body,
Of words unkindly said?

They damage you,
Hurt others,
And darken the road ahead.

When your words betray you,
No harm correcting them,
With kind ones instead.

Remember the helpers,
The energizers, the true lovers,
Who in dark times they led?

And when your soul
Was hungry for kindness,
It was them who fed?

Between your ego's self-love,
And the rights and needs of others,
Is a fine thread.

Don't be to your whims'
Destructive forces,
So closely wed.

Stay pure and polish that heart,
And use the miraculous thinking mind,
Your Lord Mercifully placed in your head.

"What Can I Say"
2018

### 3. **Inside Are Two Voices**

Inside,
Are two voices,
Dictating one,
Of two choices.

The lower voice,
Complains,
Of tests, hardships,
And pains.

The Higher Voice,
Is more graceful,
Thankful,
And Not disdainful.

The Higher Voice,
Will guide,
To contentment,
Not pride.

The lower one
Drags you down,
Don't listen,
You'll drown.

You have eyes,
Use them to see,
Don't shut them,
And create agony.

You still have time
To choose,
Which to listen to,
So you don't lose.

This is man's
Eternal fight,
Use your judgment,
And foresight.

Man's supremacy,
Is his thinking mind,
To discern between,
Being harsh or kind.

The Higher One,
Won't let you oppress,
Yourself or others
So why the stress?

Ask the source
Of Peace and Vision,
To guide you always,
To the right decision.

Inside,
Are two voices,
Dictating one,
Of two choices.

"Inside Are Two Voices"
2018

## 4. Shield Your Soul

Shield your soul,
From the poison of the unkind.
All around you,
Such people you'll find.

Their souls die,
Before they die.
Wish they knew that,
With their blind heart's eye.

Masked are their hearts,
From anything, except self-love.
Wrapped in their egos' misery,
Miles away from Heavens above.

You can smell their poison,
From far away lands.
Don't inhale it,
Bury it in the sands.

Transcend to the Healing Light,
Who will illuminate your way,
From the ugliness,
Of what they do and say.

When back,
Seek refuge with the righteous few,
Calming will be their words,
Refreshing, as morning dew.

Escape to their company,
And stay in their garden of love,
There comes your salvation,
And victory from Above.

"Shield Your Soul"
2018

## 5. Life's Swing

Don't dwell in the prison of your past,
Your now is here, for minutes it'll last.
Breathe your now all in,
Savor it, thank for it, deep down within.

Cherish what is gone,
From your story, and how it had begun,
And as you move on, dream and sing,
While riding life's unpredictable swing.

Up and down you'll swing and go,
That's how swings operate you know.
Just hold on real tight,
To those who elevate you on your flight.

Kindnesses aren't just things of your past,
They stay with you and eternally last.
They rain on you blessings from High,
In your now and after you die.

They are the jewels that beautify,
When low on your life's swing you cry.
They lift you up, again and again,
Cheering you and healing your pain.

Up on your life's swing, you'll have a blast,
But up there was never meant to last.
Prepare for your downhill slope,
Build inner strength, patience and hope.

Up and down, is your life's swing's mode,
But beautiful will be your final abode,
If kindnesses are given, seeking no reward,
Save the pleasure of your Lord.

"Life's Swing"
2018

*Inspired by one of my earliest recurring
memories: myself at three or four years
sitting one sunny morning on a swing in
the children's garden of the private club I
frequented with my family back home. My
beautiful, elegant mother, May Allah bless her
soul, full of life was giggling, as she pushed me
back and forth on the swing and her black hair
tossed away by the winds. It was exhilarating
the whole experience, she and the swing. I feel I
am still on Life's Swing, only she is not there to
push me anymore, but the memory does. Noor
Edeen our younger son, seventeen, with his
engineering mind analyzing some aspects of
the poem said, "life starts with the push from the
mother, and that push propels Life's Swing with
its ups and downs ..."*

## 6. When Love Conquers Hate Angels Are Born

When love conquers hate,
Angels are born and peace prevails,
A kind word, a good deed, a sincere smile,
A helping hand, is all it entails.

What happens, when faster than light,
From Heavens, angels descend?
Divine Protection and calm engulfs you,
If you can only comprehend.

In Heaven, angels in thousands,
Chant together, a praise symphony,
Sing along, to detoxify,
From ignorance, oppression and tyranny.

To attract them, remember Him,
And be, inside and out, fragrantly clean,
Only then, will they visit,
And you'll be rejuvenated and serene.

For earth and man, certain angels descend,
With drops of rain,
To give you life and the goodness
Of your fruit and grain.

Other angels watch over you,
As you blink, work, pray or sleep,
Some are sent to be with you,
As you rejoice or weep.

One is sent to mercifully,
Take man back to his Lord,
Easing the exit of man's soul,
To its temporary abode.

Two, record all your moves,
One on the right, for your good deeds,
And one on the left,
When your ego follows devilish needs.

Some are with you, protecting you,
Surrounding you, in all your states.
Others will greet the pious with peace,
At Heaven's gates.

Special ones are stationed,
At the gates of Hell,
They will remind its dwellers,
Of what all Prophets came to tell.

To His Will, angels submit and obey,
Unlike you,
They change shape, and from
Food and drink, they stay away.

They acknowledge heavenly knowledge,
Bestowed on them with His permission,
Hence to Him and the first man, faithfully,
They bowed in obedience and submission.

You can't find them where ugliness,
Intolerance, hate, hypocrisy, gossip
    and sin appear,
From those earthly man-made vices
They vanish and never come near.

To attract them back,
You need to look inside.
Ask yourself, what went wrong?
Keep looking, sincerely hard, till you find.

He will then move you from darknesses,
To the Light, they radiate,
That's what happens,
When you love Him and meditate.

On earth: those in remembrance and praise,
Are sought by special angels from above,
Who rejoice when they find them,
To bestow on them heavenly gifts of love.

When Love conquers hate,
Angels are born and Peace prevails.
A kind word, a good deed, a sincere smile,
A helping hand, is all it entails.

"When Love Conquers Hate, Angels Are Born"
2017

## 7. Behind Each Wrinkle Is A Story

Behind each wrinkle, is a story,
Embellished with experience's glory.

Honor each, as it appears,
Don't chill under it, with fears.

Together they sing, your own song,
A song you've lived, for so long.

They speak a language, only wrinkles
    understand,
Don't interrupt, thinking you're in command.

You are nothing but the inner shell,
On which those mighty wrinkles dwell.

Their song is silent and deeply wise,
It grows with you, as in age you rise.

They speak of your lifetime gains,
Fears, wisdoms, joys, tears and pains.

Befriend them, and tend to them with care,
For they are you, erase them, don't you dare!

Admire those hands, wrinkled with the weight,
Of lifting people, from a state to a state.

I used to look at my mother's hand,
Kiss it, for what it can withstand.

Mine, were still stretched and shiny,
Young, youthful free from agony.

Now I look at mine, and hers come to mind,
So much resemblance, I could find.

Wrinkles, they tell their own tale,
As we go from young to strong to frail.

"Behind Each Wrinkle, Is A Story"
2017

## 8

### Sincere Advice:
### Leave Your Doors Open Wide

Leave your doors open wide,
For whoever walks into your life or out.
Don't get too attached, nor too concerned.
None will stay with you except Him –
Your Eternal Mighty Friend,
Who watches over you,
Even when you sleep.
Seek His company and His pleasure,
And happiness is yours forever.
Just be cautious of "the hypocrite,
Who if he speaks, he lies,
If he promises, doesn't honor his promise,
And if trusted, he betrays."[16]

Your life tests are sent in equivalence,
To your personal power,
And to what you were designed to carry.
They are sent to test
Your power of resorting to Him,
Your patience waiting for His *Madad* -
   Divine help –
And how much trust you put
In Him Alone, all along.

---

[16] Based on a *Hadith (saying) of Prophet Muhammad, peace & blessings be upon him, pbuh,* narrated by Bukhari & Muslim.

Come close, show your poverty to Him,
Depend on Him, serve Him,
And everything beautiful will come to you.
What will be your fate if you have
All the perishable pleasures of *Dunya*,[17]
But not His pleasure? Not His mercy?
You will be quite poor and unhappy.
While if you have nothing except,
His pleasure and His mercy,
You will be the richest, the happiest,
With eternal pleasures,
And you will win the two worlds.

The choice is yours.

"Sincere Advice: Leave Your Doors Open Wide"
2017

[17]Arabic for, this world, we live in during our transient life on earth.

## 9

## One Prayer Can Change
## The Course Of Things

One prayer can change the course of things,
So if you can't fly, imagine you have wings.

You will reach far away places,
Recalling His Beautiful Names and graces.

Being truthful, humble and kind,
Will open doors, as you patiently will find.

Don't you remember when you knocked
    on His door?
And got what you asked for and even more?

So why doubt this time, you won't be heard?
Trust in no one but Him - King of the world.

Who else sees you?
All the time hears you?

"And when hungry or thirsty He feeds you?
And when sick He heals you."[18]

So why this time, He won't be with you?
Has He ever not guided you?

Keep asking, "kneel and come close"[19]
Don't drown in your own remorse.

His mansion is always open wide,
Even if your sins are far and wide.

[18] The Holy Qur'an, 26:80
[19] The Holy Qur'an, 96:19

Ask Him, repent to Him! For who is He?
The Loving One - *Al Wadud* - Who created
you and me.

"He is closer to you than your own jugular vein,"[20]
So why go far and live in pain?

Away from Him, there is no bliss,
That's a truth you should not miss.

So pack light and come, there's no time to waste,
From His Mercy and Compassion, we all crave
a taste.

Who would from The Most Serene run away?
Except if deceived by the arrogance of his
own way.

Don't fall prey to your ego's whims and
arrogance,
They are hindering forces from The Light of
His Brilliance.

Have you not seen what transpired in the past?
To egos who arrogantly lost the game so fast?

Come to The Loving One,
Who heals tired souls like none.

"To Him, The Most Beautiful Names belong,
So call on Him with those,"[21]
With their powers, you'll be forever strong.

"One Prayer Can Change The Course of Things"
2017

---

[20] The Holy Qur'an, 50:16
[21] The Holy Qur'an, 7:180

10. **Before You Complain**

Before you complain,
Look inside you and around,
He will show you His Signs,
If you truly see, you'll refrain.

Before you complain,
Contemplate others' tests
Despite yours, you are blessed,
If you truly believe, you'll refrain.

Before you complain,
Remember when you came close and asked,
Recall that answered call,
If you're grateful, you'll refrain.

Before you complain,
Think why the test?, answer is:
"Because you are loved"
If you're patient, you'll refrain.

Before you complain,
Thank instead,
Count your blessings, one by one,
If you appreciate, you'll refrain.

Before you complain,
Check who you follow,
Why inside, you feel hollow,
If you realize, you'll refrain.

Before you complain,
See who got the hardest tests?
Answer is: "His Beloveds."
If you're a beloved, you'll refrain.

Before you complain,
Ask: "Have I been with the thankful?
With the forever grateful?"
If you're in this company, you'll refrain.

Before you complain,
Rest assure He is:
The All Loving, All Knowing, All Hearing,
    All Seeing...
If you recall Those "Beautiful Names,"[22]
    you'll refrain.

Before you complain,
Ask: "How deep is my love?"
Only you and He know the answer,
Only when you love, you'll refrain.

"Before You Complain"
2017

---

[22] The Holy Qur'an, 7:180

11. **Don't Want Much**

Don't want much,
Just a Merciful touch,
Is all you need,
To be freed.

A touch of Grace,
To bless your inner space,
A helping Hand,
Across the deserts' sand.

Seek His Light,
Your only source of might,
Criticize less,
Rather your faults address.

Thank for the littlest things,
This is what happiness brings:
The joy of gratitude,
The bliss of servitude.

Read the signs sent,
As they are all meant,
To guide you through the tides,
So you run to Him in strides.

Keep Remembrance your aim,
In this life and next you'll gain.
Lighten your load,
Uphill your spiritual road.

The journey, short or long,
Needs you to be strong,
With tests, it will roughen,
Be patient, and you'll toughen.

Those on your journey, you'll meet,
Will each bring you a treat,
Sour or sweet, it'll make you wise,
Accept them all and you will rise.

"Don't Want Much"
2017

12.  ## Ignorance

The darkness of ignorance is not the problem,
The problem is staying there.

"Ignorance"
2017

13.   **Knowledge**

Ignorance is a choice we make in the face of true
Knowledge that comes our way.

"Knowledge"
2017

14. **Kindness and Contentment**

Kindness is not just in deed,
A voice can be kind,
A thought can be kind,
A glance can be kind,
A word can be kind and
A touch can be kind.
This is where warmth comes from.

Be satisfied with little to discover
    that little can be plentiful.

*AlhamdulilAllah* (Thanks to God) that my
    humble writings touch you.
They touch me too,
When I sit in the seat of the reader,
Not the author,
And from that seat,
They help me,
If you know what I mean.

"Kindness and Contentment"
2017

## 15. In and Out of Your Life

In and out of your life,
Certain people come and go.
Some love you, others shun you,
Some stay a while, while others,
depart early you know.

Miss those who passed,
For what they brought, even briefly.
Their journey was cut short,
Leaving you,
Eternally grieving deeply.

Each brings you something;
A healing word from the heart,
A wisdom, a gentle touch, a gift,
A good moment you shared,
Treasure it, before you part.

Others, intentionally or not,
Inflict on you some kind of pain,
Leaving you in fury, bewilderment,
Wondering what happened,
To make a relationship go insane.

Welcome them all.
The healers, aid you, as you go,
The others, were sent from Above,
To teach you a side of life,
To shed your skin, so you can grow.

As Joyful, tasteless or painful,
Those encounters sometimes are,
It's not by chance you had to greet them all!
Each offered you something;
A flower, a thorn or a shining star.

In any case, it's just a short journey,
We all here, on earth, share.
All we do, reflects on us eternally
Afterwards when we leave,
As we all are aware.

So be content, grateful and happy,
Shine those sentiments on others,
Love them all, for what they bring,
As that is how we heal and
Free our souls from bothers.

You will be with those you love,
Assured us the Prophet of love,
So make sure you are with
The righteous, the honorable,
And you will always be aided from Above.

"In and Out of Your Life"
2017

## 16. You Get The Picture?

A picture taken,
Is a memory from the past,
you can't relive it.

A dream anticipated,
Is a leap into the future,
you can only strive for it.

A life-giving breath,
Is your present,
Thank and enjoy it.

A foul word,
Is poison,
Stay away from it.

Let your pictures,
Reveal,
your inner goodness.

Let your dreams,
Tell,
of your greatness.

Let your breaths
Speak,
Of your gratefulness.

And let your words,
Heal,
By their sweetness.

"You Get The Picture?"
2017

## 17. Moments Worth Living

A moment in which
You lift another being,
Is a moment worth living.

A charity, sincere from the heart,
To please The Lord,
Is a charity worth giving.

A bad word followed by
A good one,
Is a word worth forgiving.

Those moments please Allah
And hence are,
Worth reliving.

Every moment that passes,
Becomes a memory,
Carved in the sands of time.

Work hard to make it
A good one for you,
Others and the world.

"Moments Worth Living"
2017

## 18. What To Do When You Don't See The Light

What to do when you don't see the Light?
Close your eyes,
And look inside.

Why is darkness the fate of some?
They see none but themselves, hear none but themselves,
Love none but themselves so in nothing but the darknesses of themselves they stay.

What happens when the self rules?
Darknesses prevails,
And the soul dies before it dies.

Why do some hate?
Because they have never,
Allowed themselves to taste love.

Where can I find the garden of love?
In the spoken word. If only the children of Adam understand,
The power of the spoken word!

Why do some get more Light than others?
Just like the earth some parts get more light than others,
It depends where you stand.

Where can I find,
The generous of this world?
Where you least expect to find them.

Who can be bathing in the sun's warmth,
And complain of the cold?
The ungrateful, who when they receive a rose
Complain of its thorns.

When is arrogance born?
When you think yourself,
A knower.

Who are the patient ones?
The ones who trust that "this too shall pass" and
Hence are thankful in times of hardships as
    well as ease.

Who are the sages of the world?
The ones who prepare ahead of time readying
Themselves and others for the ultimate journey
    back to their source.

Who do I ask for *Madad* (assistance and
    provision during my short journey)?
The Only One providing it.

How can I be happy?
Read the signs and see His Light and Beauty
    in the littlest of things,
This will transform you.

How do I earn people's love?
Bring them happiness and wipe their tears,
Even when you cry.

How do I earn His love?
Say thank you and
Be with the thankful.

Who is really blind?
"Indeed it is not the eyes, that get blind,
But it is the hearts inside that do."[23]

"What To Do, When You Don't See The Light "
2017

---

[23] The Holy Qur'an, 22:46

## 19    Let Your Soul Rule Not Your Pride

Why does man refuse to learn?
And in stubbornness, arrogance and pride,
He'd rather burn?

Does he foolishly think he knows it all?
And that he can't be educated,
From whom he perceives as insignificantly
    small?

Can't he remember,
It was Satan's pride and arrogance,
That kicked him from heaven's splendor?

O man, to rise, accept your fate,
And be unceasingly modestly thankful,
That's your passport to Heaven's gate.

Your test, is to make you humble,
Come close, acceptant, grateful,
And on Peace you will stumble.

Don't lock your heart's door from Love,
    Knowledge and Light,
And be fooled by your egoistic self,
Thinking it was you who gave you glamour
    and might.

Just remember from where these gifts came,
And being arrogantly tyrannical,
Is how you royally lose the game.

Learn the art of receiving,
Or else you'll be alone,
Eternally grieving.

When selfishness, anger and hate,
Overrides your generosity, peace and love,
Your mind will see matters, in a distorted state.

O man, lighten your load,
While you still have time,
Before you land, in your final abode.

Leave your ego on the side,
And let your soul rule,
Not your pride.

May the angels help you give birth,
To a space inside you,
Where you can find
Peace, joy and mirth.

"Let Your Soul Rule Not Your Pride"
2017

20. ## Peace Starts In The Heart

Peace starts in the heart,
Then travels to the mind,
Then in Heaven we are, in part.

That taste of Heaven,
The peaceful and content
In *dunya*, are given.

Peace follows gratitude,
Hand in hand they go together,
Cannot be without each other.

But of thanks, little we do,
Says He, Who created,
Me and you.

He promised if we thank,
He gives more and
Raises in rank.

But ungratefulness is man's own fire,
By his own hands he ignites it,
Though for peace his need is dire.

"Peace Starts In The Heart"
2017

## 21. Soul, How Deep Is Your Love

Soul, your essence is Love,
As from The Loving One's breath,
You were sent from above.

But don't you forget,
That what you think you love,
You may come to regret.

Ask then: How deep is your Love?

When it reaches its highest state,
For you, He will open,
A heavenly gate.

So why hate?
This was never meant,
To be your fate.

Instead ask: How deep is your Love?

But before, don't say "I" or "me,"
Just come, read, think, contemplate,
And you'll find the key.

Don't look further than you,
For when He loves you back,
All answers will be inside, just be true.

And you'll know: How deep is your Love.

"Soul, How Deep Is Your Love"
2017

## 22.  When Brilliance Speaks For Itself

When brilliance speaks for itself,
It silences everything else.

When gratitude fills the heart,
Love from it, will never part.

When words are uttered with love,
Angels record them from above.

When the soul sets out to serve,
Its beautiful essence it will preserve.

When from the eye, tears fall,
Watch out for an opening door.

When night's darkness takes the sun away,
Trust the promise of a new day.

When tired, seek with Him solitude,
And keep busy with His servitude.

When by His Hands you feel touched,
All your complaints must be hushed.

Then smile and be grateful,
For those are the manners of the faithful.

"When Brilliance Speaks For Itself"
2017

### 23. Amm[24] Fathi: Short Teaching Story

Often times when I lived in Cairo, Egypt, I would come back from school, and head into the elevator to go up to our apartment. With me at this time of day were always others who had also entered the elevator coming back home from work, or coming to visit someone in the building. I would always hear our elevator porter as he closed the elevator doors, call on *Allah Subhana wa Ta'ala* with those four combination of Allah's Glorious Names (Attributes), *"Ya Fatah, Ya ALeem, Ya Razak, Ya Kareem"*…..little did I know how imprinted in my subconscious those Names were and the manner with which they were said by Amm Fathi, the elevator Porter, that years later, even though I had left Egypt thirty years ago, I will be saying them in the same way in the same order, as I open my eyes every morning to start the day. Little did I know, how loaded with gifts for the day those Names were and the blessings they bring, to the one who invokes *Allah Subhana wa Ta'ala* with them. When I grew up, I realized that despite our perceived material wealth, we are all so poor *Fouqaraa*, and *Allah Subhana wa Ta'ala* Alone is the Wealthy One, *Alghanie* as we all desperately need Him and He needs none.

---

[24] Arabic word meaning literally Paternal uncle, but used with older men who come from a modest background as a title before their name, out of respect.

Sheikh Muzaffer Ozak explains:

"Ya Fatah: The Opener, He Who opens the
solution to all problems and makes things
easy. Repetition of this Name brings
openness of heart and opens doors.

Ya ALeem: The All Knowing: He Who has
full knowledge of all things. Our hearts are
illuminated by invoking this glorious Name
and many qualities of light will shine from
within us.

Ya Razaak: The Provider: He Who provides
all things useful to His servants. Gates of
providence are open for those who call on
Allah with this Name.

Ya Karem: The Most Generous: He Whose
generosity is unmatchable. Those who
constantly invoke this glorious Name will be
esteemed in this world and the next."[25]

Thank You *Amm Fathi*, May God bless his soul.
He taught me a lot without knowing it.

"Amm Fathi: Short teaching Story"
2017

[25] Al-Jerrahi, Muzaffer O. *Irshad: Wisdom of a Sufi Master*. New York: PIR Press,
1988. Print.

### 24. With The Break Of Dawn

With the break of dawn,
New beginnings,
Are in full bloom.

So when angelic birds,
Wake you up, with their healing song,
Rise, praise, and chant along.

And when the lover utters
One word, from his heart, listen well,
It has passages of gifts for you.

And if your heart,
With problems hurt,
Praise the Lord and do not divert.

Let goodness be your charm,
And wherever you go,
Spread peace and calm.

Make friends who see,
Love, As the way to be,
Those will last, and won't flee.

Cherish them, hug them,
With your soul serve them,
For that's how lovers are meant to be.

"With The Break of Dawn"
2016

### 25. What Happened To Our Earth

I feel such pain,
Everywhere I look.
What would anyone gain,
diverting so much from the Book.

What happened to our earth?
It is on fire!
With hatred, greed and a rebirth,
Of every ugly desire.

With raised hands and tears,
I ask for *Madad*[26] from The One,
Who can transform greed, sadness and fears,
To kindness, peace and love, like none.

Our Lord, please accept our prayers,
For a safe passage from this test.
Our sadness inside is heavy in layers,
Robbing every moment of rest.

In You we trust,
As there is no other,
Who can cleanse hearts from rust,
To help us save one another.

"What Happened to Our Earth"
2016

[26] An Arabic term for seeking Divine support & assistance

## 26.    O My Dear Sun

Where will you go,
O my dear sun,
When you leave,
My field of vision?

You are my light,
You are my warmth,
How will I live,
When I am not in your presence?

I know you will come back,
To shine on me again,
But the night is long, cold,
and chilly, without you to behold.

Parting with you,
Means letting go,
Of my soul,
So you can grow.

But my heart will always sense,
When you're having a cloudy day.
My only wish then,
Is not to be, half the world away.

I trust you will rise,
High above my expectations,
O my dear sun,
Just remember I will be forever waiting.

"O My Dear Sun"
2015

## 27. A Lone Tree I Stand

A lone tree I stand,
Facing the turbulent
Winds of time,
In fury and frenzy
They toss and turn,
Yet in my cooling loving shade,
A calming serenade,
Is heard.

Healing as it may be,
Yet from it, they flee,
To where?
Don't ask me,
For I am only,
That lone standing tree,
Facing the turbulent
Winds of time.

My roots are firm,
Into the ground.
My branches spread out
And touch the sky,
And ask, to make us,
Keep standing strong
Facing the turbulent
Winds of time.

"A Lone Tree I Stand"
2015

### 28.   Only When[27]

Only when you see trials,
As Allah's Divine means,
Of your purification in *dunya*,
Will you welcome them,
More readily.

Only when you come to Him,
Devoid of all worldly loves,
That weigh on you, heavy,
Will you enter into His Presence,
And feel light.

Only when you sincerely seek,
Him Alone,
Who can lift all your burdens,
Instantly, with His *Madad*
Will you be cured.

Only when you consciously,
Submit to His will,
Knowing His plan for you,
Is the best,
Will you be content.

Only when you look inside,
And settle accounts,
With yourself and others,
Will your soul,
Be happy and free.

[27] Hamed, Maissa M. "Only When" *The Muslim Woman Magazine.* 10, Nov. 2017: Vol 18. Print.

Only when you serve joyfully,
Lifting people up,
Wiping the tears of the suffering,
Will you be blessed and
Gain heavenly Jewels.

Only when your kindness,
Overrides your anger,
Which can destroy you,
Will you feel at peace,
With yourself and others.

Only when you 'read'
His heavenly and worldly books,
Will you see His Signs,
Which are all,
Around and in you.

Only when you start your day,
Grateful you were granted,
Yet another chance,
While others weren't,
Will you appreciate it,
And make the best of it.

Only when you live life, certain,
That He is looking at
Your heart and deeds,
Will you be cleansed inside
And beautified.

Only when you worship Him,
Not, so He gives,
But, so He is pleased,
Will you get,
Endlessly from His Bounty.

Only when you wake up,
To the beauty of Love,
Will you follow, out of love,
And be transformed,
And loved.

Only when you realize,
You own nothing, and everything
You have, including you,
Belongs to Him,
Will you be thankful.

Only when you sit and learn,
From those who radiate His Light,
Will you shine,
And learn,
The language of love.

Only when your love to His beloved
Exceeds all your other loves, except Him,
Will you be enlightened,
And cleansed to enter,
The Garden of love.

Only when you come close,
With the right etiquette,
Will you be allowed in the garden,
And will drink,
From His oceans of mercy.

Only when you know,
That you leave, with nothing but,
Your words and deeds,
Will you become aware,
Of how to be human.

Only when you listen well,
To your heart,
When it knocks on the door of Love,
And loses itself inside,
Will you be guided.

Only when you visit your grave,
Will you know,
What kind of palace,
You spent,
Your whole life building.

"Only When"
2015

## 29. An Open Dome To Heaven

When the spiritual and technological combine,
With the latter serving the former,
The resulting experience,
Is utterly divine.

*Medinah*, city of Prophet Muhammad, pbuh
Is full of grace.
Where he rests, became a great mosque,
    a haven,
So majestic and a beloved sacred place.

Everyone who goes
To bid him greetings of *'Salam'*,[28]
Returns, a storyteller and knows,
He's been touched by the spirit of Islam
And its great *Imam*.

My short visit,
Was no exception.
So tangible is the presence of the
    Prophet's spirit,
Greeting you in every direction.

Before dawn, one blessed April morning,
I sat, under a dome, meditating in a free
    quiet spot.
Soon, many came flocking in early,
    like me, yearning,
Despite the weather which was getting
    quite hot.

---

[28] Arabic for Peace, one of Allah's *Subhana wa Ta'ala* Divine Names.

The numbers started to increase steadily,
As the congregational dawn prayer approached.
The eclectic energy of diverse visitors was
    felt readily,
Who on my free space gradually encroached.

I started to feel the heat,
As I sat under the dome.
The air inside seemed deplete.
What to do? Do I stand up and roam?

No, I decided to stay.
With raised hands and eyes towards the
    hidden sky,
I started to pray,
For a cool breeze to nourish us all, from up
    high.

Miraculously, as I finished my prayer request,
The dome, separating me from the Heavens
    above,
Started sliding, reclining, creating an opening,
I thought 'what a Heavenly gest
That cool breeze that embraced us all, with
    Love.'

A sublime moment of a prayer immediately
    fulfilled,
Left me in absolute awe,
Through a technology so skilled,
Which I admit, I never before saw.

I attempted to capture,
A moment so thrilling.
This open dome to Heaven, left me in such
    rapture,
O my! How fulfilling!

The courtyard gradually became more bright,
As a sweet breeze, through it, swept.
The open dome to Heaven brought "Light
    upon Light,"[29]
A sacred engineering so new,
Designed by a blessed gifted few.

"An Open Dome To Heaven"
2015

---

[29] The Holy Qur'an, 24:35.

30. **Just Serve**

Just serve,
If it is your wealth,
Give, to multiply it.

Just serve,
If it is your thought,
Speak, and beautify it.

Just serve,
If it is your pen,
Write, and sanctify it.

Just serve,
If it is your heart,
In Prayer, occupy it.

"Just Serve"
2015

## 31. A Light Guest

A light guest,
Shined on my wall,
Stayed a while and left,
Couldn't see it any more.

I will always remember it,
Vivid, elegant and clear,
That blend of all colors,
So beautiful, O dear!

Every day, I yearn,
As I start my day,
Will it ever return?
Or has it gone its own way?

Lucky me,
To have witnessed its short presence,
To have been able to see,
Beauty in all its essence.

"A Light Guest"
*In memory of my beloved mother.*
2015

32.   **Farewell Bibou**[30]

I don't know
Where to start.
I'm in awe,
Ripped apart.

Bibou, how fast,
Was your return!
After a past,
Of love, at every turn.

Your infectious smile,
Still echoes in the land,
Your lovable, huggable style,
Was your unique brand.

*Zarzour & Ismaeen*[31] portray
The truly funny, gifted you,
Who genuinely and every day,
Uplifted everyone he knew.

O sweet, content soul,
We bid you farewell,
With our prayers,
That in eternal bliss, you dwell.

Remember how with dBase,
Waks[32], you and I had a blast?
When you helped with my thesis analysis,
Though with math, I'm far from fast!

---

[30] Tarek Labib, nicknamed *Bibou*, more than a brother to my husband and me. His sudden death, left many deeply grieving.

[31] Fictional characters he used to, may he rest in peace, allude to in his jokes.

[32] My husband's nick name, short for Mohamed Elwakil.

You left us your home -
An architect's masterpiece -
Standing all alone,
In beauty, serenity and peace.

I suggest it be a Museum
To celebrate,
A lovely soul,
And its gifted vision.

So long, our dearest brother and friend,
Loved and missed already by all,
As a sign of Allah's love,
To this beautiful, gifted soul.

*In memory of our lovely brother Tarek Labib,*
*May his sweet soul rest in eternal peace.*

"Farewell Bibou"
2015

**You Can Only Fill An Empty Vessel**

You can only fill
An empty vessel,
Can it receive,
If it is full?

It is only in silence,
That you can talk to Him.
So be silent often,
And search within.

It is because of day,
That we know night.
So have a sip of love,
And you'll never fight.

It is because of life,
That we know death.
It all started,
With His breath.

It is our deeds,
That can lift,
Not our creeds,
So make the shift.

It is because of pain,
That we know joy,
For they are opposite sides
Of the same coin.

Remember that He twice said,
In his Glorious Book;
"With adversity, comes prosperity."[33]

So trust that
"This too will pass"
And with patience,
We rise to another class.

"You Can Only Fill An Empty Vessel"
2014

### 34. Come To The Gardens Of Love

Close your eyes,
So you can see,
Inside.

Halt that tongue,
So you can listen well,
To your heart.

Cry it all out,
If need be,
To be happy and free.

Race fast towards goodness,
Before you lose the race,
With time, the fastest runner.

Calm that brain,
So you can listen,
To the birds' healing songs.

Give, even the littlest thing,
From what you love,
So you can be rich.

Know Love,
For it is the only,
Eternal Truth.

Be light,
So you can,
Fly.

See beauty,
For it is all around
You.

Enjoy some solitude,
For in it,
Is your recharge.

Serve others,
For that is the way of the righteous,
To eternal bliss.

Look up to the Heavens and dream,
It may come true,
For you are always heard.

Trust,
That you are never alone,
In His presence.

Choose your companions,
For you will become,
Who you are with.

Rearrange those verses,
If you so desire, they all stand alone,
As we all will.

Who am I,
To tell you all this,
I think you know it all.

The list is long,
Keep thinking
For contemplation is worship.

Come
To the gardens of Love,
And you will be healed.

"Come To The Gardens Of Love"
2014

### 35.   My Bike and I

My bike and I,

Are best friends forever.
We journey life together,
Thru smooth and bumpy terrain,
Sometimes parting,
Before reuniting,
Again.

My bike and I,

Go fast and sometimes slow,
On light snow,
In the sun or shade,
To quietly de-stress,
From a worldly mess,
To our finely tuned serenade.

My bike and I,

Wonder thru the streets,
Hearing singing birds and their tweets.
Oftentimes, with the wind's grace,
We smell the flowers' fragrant smell,
And the freshness of the grass they dwell,
As we go slow or sometimes race.

My bike and I,

Relish going on two wheels!
You've got to try it, know how exhilarating
    it feels,
In city, desert or seascape,
When the wind blows your troubles away,
You rejuvenate in a spectacular way,
And you return in much better shape.

My bike and I,

Often meet other bikers on the road,
Traveling with us, in the same mode.
A mutual sigh of joy is the effect,
Whether we stop to greet or not,
Inside we feel that little jolt,
Signaling mutual respect.

My bike and I,

Head forward in time or back,
Like in a movie or sound track,
With dreams and memories,
That fill each ride,
Thru the tide,
With relaxing melodies.

My bike and I,

Always on the go,
In a hurry or slow,
We get errands done:
Fruits, freshly baked bread,
Flowers or a fine cheese spread,
Then home, after thanking everyone.

My bike and I,

Take off momentarily, leaving troubles behind,
To a serene spot, that we can find,
For moments of reflection and contemplation.
Only from that station, that we see
Differently, the situation we flee
And the solution comes, with consolation.

My bike and I,

Are happy to live healthy,
As happy, doesn't necessarily come from
    wealthy!
But happy, is a state of mind,
Search for it, all your life,
Away from anger, hatred, jealousy and strife,
Look for it well, and you will find.

My bike and I,

Bid you now farewell.
Gratitude to Allah for each moment,
We live healthy and well.
That grateful feeling, keeps us going,
And in a healthy, grateful mode of love,
We thank and seek help from Above,
For He alone, is the All Knowing.

"My Bike and I"
2014

### 36. Foolish Is He

Foolish is he,
Who gives up Heavenly treasures,
For earthly ones.

Poor is he,
Whose love of money,
Delivers him to all sorts of evil.

Sick is he,
Who takes greed,
As his master.

Lost is he,
Who becomes a slave,
To his ego.

Ignorant is he,
Who knows not, that greed is a trap,
That brings ruin and destruction.

Blind is he,
Who knows not,
Which master is worthy of worship.

"Hypocrite is he
Who speaks not
What is in his heart."[34]

---

[34] Hadith of Prophet Muhammad, pbuh.

"Unthankful to God is he,
who has not
thanked people."[35]

Proud is he,
Who when wrong,
Does not repent.

Stubborn is he,
Who refuses The Light,
And insists on his darknesses.

Deceived is he,
Who forgets,
What true love, is all about.

Dead is he,
Who lives life,
Forgetting how to be human.

Tormented is he,
Who wakes up late,
And misses the heavenly train.

"Foolish Is He"
2014

---

[35] Hadith of Prophet Muhammad, pbuh.

37.   **This Time I Cried**

This time I cried,
As I boarded the plane,
In my heart,
Layers of pain,
As Egypt crosses,
Dangerous terrain.
But I trusted,
Never doubted
Egypt will rise again.

In glory,
It will always stand.
How not?
When numerous Prophets with Allah's
     command,
Treaded its precious sand,
Leaving on its people eternal traces,
And blessing its Nile and land
With Allah's *Subhana wa Ta'ala* Graces.

Deep down,
I know,
This will pass,
Despite,
Expectations, not met,
Deaths, hard to forget,
Fuel, a rare commodity,
Traffic, suffocating a community,
And a revolution sabotaged.

Because it is the Egyptians' patience,
That yields them extra courageous,
In the face of trials.
Historically, O look,
How many we passed,
With determination and unity,
We surpassed,
The Brits, the French,
And many others in our rich past.

June 30 is fast approaching,
With many in power, stubbornly encroaching,
On the right of Egypt,
To belong to its people.
To the street again,
Every Egyptian will go.
Not just to Tahrir Square,
This time you'll see them everywhere.
United and full of determination,
To take back their country,
Peacefully, no confrontation.

To them all,
Egyptian women, men and children,
We raise our hands in prayer and meditation,
Asking for a Divine lifting,
Of this situation,
That has left
Our country shaking,
Our economy aging,
Our systems failing,
And our souls yearning,
For a Divine intervention,
That is the intention.

May Allah the Almighty
Send hosts of angels as aids,
To carry Egypt peacefully,
Through His Heavenly gates,
And raise its beautiful people,
To the highest of states.

"This Time I Cried"
2013

## 38. A New Year Wish

Last week, before 2004 ended,
Millions of people and whole communities
    surrendered,
To the worst tsunami ever recorded.
The Indian Ocean's floor suddenly shifted,
Creating gigantic deadly waves that
    powerfully drifted,
Slamming shores of fifteen countries,
Leaving them horrendously affected.

This event has touched me so deep,
As I see millions weep,
And drown into the ocean deep,
Into a deep, deep sleep.
Devastated and wrecked,
Asia and the world,
Experienced a calamity,
That was hard to expect.
It's not yet Judgment Day,
But to many, it felt that way.
The outbreak of money, supplies and
    donations continued to pour,
But could not match the devastation
And bodies on shore.

The trivialities of my life problems. O!
How small they now should be,
After the destruction, my eyes could see.
Thank God, I have a family and a modest
    home to stay,
Millions lost it all, close ones, homes,
And all they worked for to this day!

In comparison, I dare not say,
That I have any problems today!
Nor can I imagine myself, in such a disarray.
All of a sudden, I felt my problems, fade away,
As I think of the victims, the dead, and the
    homeless.
I realize how in the face of death,
We are utterly helpless,
The afterlife is so near,
O Dear,
So let us all strive to become,
The best a human being could be,
Before it is too late, to do, to act or to see.
May Allah *subhana wa Ta'ala* help
    them all,
Dead, alive, wounded, distressed they may be.
That is a New Year wish from me.

"A New Year Wish"
2005

## 39.  My Diamond Earring

Two days ago,
I lost my diamond earring in the snow!
All of a sudden, just like my mother,
*Allah Subhana wa Ta'ala* decided, it should go.

It was originally hers, you know,
Day and night I wore it, for six years or so,
For it always reminded me of my mother,
And that's why losing it, is a real bother.

I went looking for it in the street,
With snow all the way up to my feet,
And there was a man who I was to meet,
His face was charming and really sweet,
Who watered the pavement, so it's nice
    and neat.

I told him I wish he didn't,
As now the earring got buried more deep.
He told me, "Tonight, I will look for
    your earring,
And if I find it, to you I will bring it,
But bring it where?"
I told him I lived over there,
Across the street from where we were.

I had tears in my eyes,
And he told me, "Don't cry,
For when it gets dry,
Maybe we'll find it, all we could do is try."
At this point, I was really sad,
And I just wished that my Dad,
Was here to comfort me with a shoulder pat.

But my two children were here,
So sad they were, to see my tear.
So I went home and prayed,
And I felt better no more dismayed,
That my husband and two children were saved,
And that it was only a diamond earring,
That I lost in the snow.

"My Diamond Earring"
2004

## 40. Birth and Death

Birth and death,
And the passage of breath,
From womb to tomb,
It travels fast,
As no one is here to last,
Except *Allah Subhana wa Ta'ala The Almighty*
Who in a blast,
Created a world so vast.

But who are we to think,
That even for one blink,
We can have a say,
In His plans for us, everyday.

In a moment, a child is born,
In another, a heart is torn.
No matter what, we can never know,
What He has for us in store.
But one has to trust and keep in the fore,
The truth, that He knows best.
Hence His Will, we have to always accept,
Trust, and to it submit,
In gratitude and respect.

And in the midst of life,
With all its bliss and strife,
One should never lose sight,
Of the transience of our earthly life,
For in a moment, a child is born
And in another a heart is torn.

"Birth and Death"
2000

*From One Lover's Heart to Another: Forty Sufi Poems*

# ABOUT THE AUTHOR

Maissa Hamed is an Egyptian American poet, author, educator, researcher, educational curriculum developer, storyteller, designer, photographer and Islamic Calligraphy student of Master Calligrapher Mohamed Zakariya. Maissa uses poetry to weave in subtly embedded Islamic wisdoms and mystical teachings for the benefit of her students and audiences which she threads together drawing on the teachings of the Qur'an and the Ahadith of Prophet Muhammad, *Salla Allahu alayhee wa sallam, Peace & Blessings be upon him, pbuh.*

A former staff member of UNICEF, she has over thirteen years national and international experience in program and policy development, focusing on child labor and education in developing countries, child rights advocacy, research and social mobilization. In 1989, she represented the Middle East Region in Geneva as member, UNICEF's delegation to the final drafting of the UN Convention on the Rights of the Child – the fastest ratified human rights treaty in history. In 1995, she co-managed UNICEF's first on-line youth mobilization campaign where, for the first time, UNICEF led the UN in soliciting worldwide youth participation in policy planning at the World Summit for Social Development voicing their ideas on poverty eradication, unemployment and social conflict to Heads of State attending the summit.

Maissa is a New York-based Freelance Education and Research Consultant for Sesame Workshop, where since 1998 she worked with Sesame

Workshop's International Research Department on several international researches, as well as educational curriculum content development and script reviews in conjunction with international co-productions. She also provided consulting services for Scholastic, the Metropolitan Museum of Art, The Rudolf Steiner School of New York among other schools in the New York area, Games Productions and MediaKidz Research and Consulting.

In 2006, she founded Enjoy Islam—The first spiritual educational teaching methodology to adapt Waldorf teaching philosophies and techniques to a uniquely designed Islamic and Arabic language curriculum that guides, enriches, transforms and inspires seekers of all ages, to progress on their spiritual journey, building on the power of knowledge and love to purify hearts and utilizing the ancient Arab traditions of poetry, storytelling and calligraphy. Enjoy Islam is an artistically creative, educational and spiritual endeavor which brings true knowledge of Islam and its arts and culture to American families.

In 2007, Steiner Books published her first book, *The Last Night of Ramadan* as the first of the Enjoy Islam book series.

In April 2013, in conjunction with the Metropolitan Museum of Art's newly inaugurated Arab and Islamic galleries, Maissa was invited as Master Calligrapher to participate in planning and implementing the Islamic calligraphy segment and to conduct a story telling segment for children and families in Arabic and English for the family day: *Senses of Springtime.*

Maissa participated in several interfaith events, has several published poems, articles, papers, reports, and participated in numerous conferences and seminars including radio and TV interviews.

Maissa has a B.A. in psychology and an M.A. in social sciences from The American University, Cairo. She lives in New York City with her husband, Architect Mohamed El Wakil, AIA, and their two sons. She is a member of the Academy of American Poets, The League of American Bicyclists and a former member of Rudolf Steiner School's Diversity Committee and Parents Council, where she is yearly invited as a guest lecturer.

# GLOSSARY

*Al-Aleem*

> The All-Knowing - One of Allah's Ninety-Nine 'Beautiful Names' mentioned in the Holy Qur'an. Muslims invoke The Names in private or collectively in Sufi Dhikr gatherings. Allah *Subhana wa Ta'ala* in the Holy Qur'an invites believers to call on Him with Those Names, as they are of tremendous spiritual, psychological and healing powers.

*Al Burda of Al Busiri*

> *Al Burda* or *The Cloak* is the renowned Arabic poem or *Qasida* of the Thirteenth Century Arabic Sufi Poet, Imam Al-Busiri, who held several positions in *Mamluk* Egypt and wrote it in praise of Prophet Muhammad's impeccable character and exemplary traits. The story goes that Imam Al-Busiri developed a kind of paralysis in half his body that left him immobile. So he prayed intensely asking for Divine Healing and for the intercession of the Prophet. He wrote his poem and emotionally kept repeating it praising the Prophet and asking for his intercession so that Allah *Subhana wa Ta'ala* Heals him. When Imam Al-Busiri slept that night, Prophet Muhammad, pbuh, appeared to him in a dream and with his blessed hand gently covered the paralyzed Imam with his blessed cloak, *Al-Burda*. Imam Al-Busiri woke up from his miraculous dream to find that his prayer was granted with the intercession of the

Prophet and he was totally healed! *Al-Burda* is memorized by millions and chanted in musical congregations in honour of the Prophet till today all over the Muslim world. Its stanzas are of great spiritual significance and were translated into over ten languages.

*Al-Fatah*
> The Opener - One of Allah's 'Beautiful Names'.

*Al-Ghanie*
> The Wealthy, Self-Sufficient One - One of Allah's 'Beautiful Names'.

*Al-Kareem*
> The Generous - One of Allah's 'Beautiful Names'.

*Al-Razak*
> The Provider, The Sustainer - One of Allah's 'Beautiful Names'.

*Al-Wadud*
> The Loving One - One of Allah's 'Beautiful Names'.

*AlhamdulilAllah*
> Thanks be to God.

*Allah*
> God.

Amm
> Literally means paternal uncle. A title used with older men of modest background out of respect, so as not to call them directly by their first name.

Book
Holy Scripture, Divine Revelation.

Dervish
A Sufi.

*Dhikr*
Remembrance of God in private or collectively as a group.

*Dunya*
The material transient world, our earthly existence.

Ego
Lower self.

Final Day
Day of judgment or resurrection.

*Fouqaraa*
The Poor. Sufis acknowledge their spiritual poverty/need for Allah *Subhana wa Ta'ala* at all times, despite any perceived material wealth.

*Hadith*
Sayings of Prophet Muhammad pbuh. *Hadith* (singular) or *Ahadith* (plural) are short written accounts of the words and actions of the Prophet, in almost any given situation which have been carefully recorded by his companions to keep his *sunna* - Prophetic traditions - alive after him. Together the science of Hadith and the Holy Qur'an constitute the two main sources of guidance for Muslims. The Ahadith are authenticated by narrators and traced back

to the Prophet, through a detailed chain of transmission.

He/Him

Used in the Holy Qur'an to refer to God.

*Imam*

Leader of a congregational prayer, and/or a Muslim scholar.

*Islam*

Submission to God. The religion of Islam is based on the teachings of Prophet Muhammad, pbuh - seal of Prophets - as per the Holy Qur'an, which is the final unchanged Word of God, revealed to the Prophet by Angel Gabriel over a period of twenty-three years.

*Madad*

A call on Allah *Subhana wa Ta'ala* seeking Divine support.

*Mamluks*

Under the Sultans of the *Mamluk* Dynasty (1250–1517), who were great patrons of the arts and architecture, Cairo became the intellectual, cultural and artistic capital of the Muslim world. Sufism was part of the spiritual fabric of life in Egypt and Syria and "outstanding architectural innovations especially in mosque architecture were made."[36] Artisans produced Islamic decorative arts of exquisite superior quality examples of which still stand till today, which impacted

[36] Frishman, Martin, and Khan, Hasan-Uddin, editors. *The Mosque: History, Architectural Development & Regional Diversity.* Cairo:The American University in Cairo Press, 2002.

international trade and local production in Europe. "The influence of *Mamluk* glassware on the Venetian glass industry is one such example."[37]

*Meccan*

Of or related to the Holy city of Mecca - birth place of Prophet Muhammad pbuh.

*Medinah*

The second holiest city in Islam after Mecca, originally known as *Yathrib*. After the Prophet's death it became known as *Al Madinah Al Munawarra* - The Illuminated City.

*Muslim*

A follower of Prophet Muhammad pbuh, and the religion of Islam.

*Qur'an*

The last of God's Holy Scriptures to humanity – the Qur'an - is the Holy book of Muslims, the unchanged Word of God revealed to Prophet Muhammad, pbuh, through Angel Gabriel - as a guidance for humanity.

*Ramadan*

The blessed ninth month of the Islamic lunar calendar in which the first words of the Holy Qur'an were revealed to Prophet Muhammad, pbuh. A month whereby Muslims fulfill the obligation of fasting daily from dawn to sundown in order to gain a renewed state of God-consciousness in every word and deed hence developing a much needed closeness

[37] https://www.metmuseum.org/toah/hd/maml/hd_maml.htm. The reader is referred to the Met's exhibition catalogue: *Venice and the Islamic World* for further readings on the subject.

to their Creator. It is customary for devout Muslims to read the entire Qur'an during the month and reflect on the life story of The Prophet in an attempt to keep his *sunna* alive in their hearts during *Ramadan* and well beyond.

*Salam*

Peace, the first word of the traditional greeting in Islam.

*Salla Allahu alayhee wa sallam*

Peace and Blessings of Allah upon him.

*Shaykh*

Title used for an old man of wisdom. In Sufism, the title is used for the Sufi teacher who has *murids* - students.

*Sohba*

A spiritual talk given by a Sufi teacher. It also means companionship.

*Subhana wa Ta'ala*

Traditional magnification following God's Name, meaning 'Praise be to Allah, The Most Exalted.'

*Sufi*

A devout Muslim taught by a Sufi Shaykh the mystical path of Islam where devotion to God is based on the love of *Allah Subhana wa Ta'ala*, the love of Prophet Muhammad, pbuh, purification of the heart by seeking a state of God-consciousness at all times in private and public in all thoughts, words, actions and sincerity in following the *sunna* of Prophet Muhammad, *pbuh*, - the ultimate exemplar.

*Sunna*
The Prophetic Traditions of Prophet Muhammad, pbuh, which guide Muslims in every aspect of their daily lives, behaviours and interactions with others and which is based on the Holy Qur'an.

# BIBLIOGRAPHY

Al-Jerrahi, Muzaffer O. *Irshad: Wisdom of a Sufi Master.* New York: PIR Press, 1988.

Atiyeh, Al-Kindi. "Rasa'il al-Kindi al-Falsafiya." *www.muslimheritage.com.* Rawalpindi: Islamic Research Institute, 1966, p. 127.

Carboni, Stefano, ed. *Venice and the Islamic World, 828–1797.* Exhibition catalogue. New Haven: Yale University Press, 2007.

Frishman, Martin, and Khan, Hasan-Uddin, editors. *The Mosque: History, Architectural Development & Regional Diversity.* Cairo: The American University in Cairo Press, 2002.

Garda, Yusuf C. *Literature, Life and Cricket: Tales of Fietas.* Cape Town: African Lives in Association with the Gauteng Cricket Board, 2017.

Hamed, Maissa. Illustrated by Elwakil, Mohamed. *The Last Night of Ramadan.* Great Barrington: Bell Pond Books, 2007.

Hamed, Maissa M. "Only When" The Muslim Woman Magazine. 10, Nov. 2017: Vol 18.

Hamid, Ahmad & Hamed, Mohamed. *Meaning of the Holy Qur'an translated into English.* Cairo: Dar El Shorouk, 2011. Print. Read more *http://enjoyislam.net/quran_in_rhyme.html*

Yalman, Suzan. "The Art of the Mamluk Period (1250 –1517)." In *Heilbrunn Timeline of Art History.* New York: The Metropolitan Museum of Art, 2000–. *http://www.metmuseum.org/toah/hd/ maml/hd_maml.htm* (October 2001)

Wordsworth, William Quotes. "BrainyQuote.com. Xplore Inc, 2018. 14 May 2018. *https://www.brainyquote.com/quotes/william_ wordsworth_390135*

*Notes*

# Notes

*From One Lover's Heart to Another: Forty Sufi Poems*